The Denton Connection

Stan Weeber
Department of Social Science
McNeese State University

THE DENTON CONNECTION

On the afternoon of November 22, 1963, Robert Oswald was working at the Acme Brick Company just off the Stemmons Freeway in Denton, Texas, about 35 miles northwest of Dealey Plaza. Upon hearing that his brother Lee Oswald had been arrested in the shooting of a policeman, Robert asked his superiors for time off to attend to his brother in Dallas. Bob Oswald would stay away from Denton for eight days, and he had no idea how his neighbors would react upon his return. As it turned out, there was no cause for alarm. The Oswalds received no crank calls or threatening mail.[1] The local press was most kind: only a mercifully short piece on the next to last page of the November 24 *Denton Record-Chronicle* verified that Oswald and his family lived in the city.[2] Reporters described Oswald as a decent, hardworking man caught up in an unfortunate situation.[3] Later, after the FBI had thoroughly checked Oswald out, Denton police quietly spread the word among the townsfolk that

Robert was "all right," and had nothing to do with the assassination.[4]

Dentonites prefer that this humane, down-home portrait of neighborly concern for the accused assassin's brother be the one that people think of when a "Denton Connection" to the assassination of President Kennedy is mentioned. They also prefer that the city's brief encounter with Robert Oswald be "the end" of the city's association with the President's murder.[5]

Over the years researchers have come across many more bits and pieces linking events in Denton, or Dentonites (current or former) to the assassination. When I speak of the Denton Connection, I mean some evidentiary strands that have not been woven together until now. Some strands are important because of the leads they produce – for instance, I will identify a "White Alliance" of Birchist college students in the city that merits further examination in light of the evidence linking rightists/neo-Nazis to the assassination.[6]

Other strands that are part of the tapestry are interesting because of what they say about how and why significant evidence in the JFK case has been suppressed at the local level. I view Denton as a case study in this suppression process. I believe that Denton hoped to avoid at all costs the adverse economic impact that a fully developed and publicized Denton Connection would have produced. The city succeeded in suppressing its ties to the assassination via a conspiracy of silence, a plot that was "from above," or elite-driven, as well as "from below." Dentonites of all social classes tacitly encouraged the cover-up that has hindered our efforts to find the truth. The extremely conservative political orientation of Denton's citizens led them to buy into the cover-up rather than to challenge it. This cover-up continues in Denton today just as it did over 50 years ago when it first began.

The Denton Connection is also significant because certain key Dentonites helped to shape what we learned about the assassination in the critical days and weeks after the event, and what interpretation was given to the knowledge that had been constructed. I will argue that the city's conservatism had a very strong influence on the gathering of this knowledge as well as its interpretation. Denton cannot, of course, take the full blame for the stonewalling of information or evidence in the JFK case that has occurred throughout the United States and the world. That cover-up is a larger structural problem and one that likely has its roots in the highest officials of the federal government. But the actions of principal Dentonites nonetheless played into the hands of the conspirators. Most of the nation accepted for two years the information constructed and relayed by Dentonites from Dallas, Washington, and elsewhere, while the trail that led to the conspirators grew colder by the day.

Protecting Dynamic Denton

The cover-up in Denton was perpetuated for the rawest of economic reasons: to avoid the negative publicity from the more negative Denton connections that would end up hurting the economy of this fledgling, yet growing North Texas community.

"Dynamic Denton" was the slogan adopted by the local Board of Realtors in the mid-Sixties to entice businesses and families to move to this small city in the North Texas Cotton Belt.[7] Certainly, something did entice people to move to Denton even before the Dynamic Denton campaign started, as witnessed by the town's transformation from a sleepy agricultural trading center into a diversified industrial city of 27,000 by 1961.[8] Local Realtors attributed the growth to the city's small town atmosphere and its proximity to major urban trappings in Dallas and Fort Worth. Further, Denton's "university community" – the town was home to two postsecondary schools with a combined enrollment of 11,000 in 1961 – gave the small place a certain cosmopolitan ambiance that cities of comparable size did not have.[9]

For all the progress that had been made in the decades leading up to the Sixties, Denton's economic future in 1963 was quite shaky. The city was at a crossroads, not knowing if it could develop a legitimate identity in its own right, or if it would be relegated forever to "stepchild" status in relation to the rapidly growing Dallas-Fort Worth metroplex.[10]

To publicly acknowledge Denton's possible connections to the assassination would have thrown a major wrench into the gears of economic progress that were churning steadily forward at the time. The economic impact of the murder upon Dallas, though never systematically measured that I know of, must have been staggering. Hundreds of businesses undoubtedly chose not to relocate to the city or hold conventions or meetings there. Conventions already scheduled for the city in 1964 may have been canceled after November 22. There was enough concern about the economy in Dallas that Dallasites wondered if the economic growth of their city would come to an end.[11] The city fathers of Denton were similarly business-minded and wanted to avoid that predicament for their city. The old money elitists that dominated Denton's politics and government, and who essentially "ran things" in 1963 by virtue of their ownership or control of the local factories and newspapers, made a decision to downplay the Robert Oswald connections, and all the others, primarily for economic reasons. We cannot infer this solely from informants or long-secret "smoking gun" documents because small towns do not produce either resource in large quantities. We know this mostly from the behavior of the city's residents both before and after the assassination.[12]

Simply put, the city stonewalled the Denton Connection. The city's gentle treatment of the Oswalds appeared to be genuine neighborliness on the surface, and to a certain extent it was, but it was just a veneer overlaying certain basic economic facts of life. Continuation of the stonewalling into the new millennium suggests that the city fathers still fear that bad publicity from the Kennedy assassination will be bad for Denton's businesses.

The unabashed civic boosterism of the Chamber of Commerce and the Board of Realtors in most Southern cities masked a dark side of the towns' history that was mostly unreported and stood in stark counterpoint to the rosy picture painted by the business crowd. An outward manifestation of this dark side was displayed in 1963 and 1964 during the efforts in Congress to pass a Civil Rights Act. Southerners resisted the idea that minorities should be given the same rights as white citizens as prescribed by the Act. To do so, they argued, would go against the freedom of the local businessmen to run their businesses as they choose.[13] Underneath the surface of genteel society, there was an unspoken tolerance of repressive, terroristic actions upon those who were fighting for their constitutional rights.[14] This violent history went unreported in Denton as it did throughout the South.[15] And the denial of the dark side was, I believe, performed for the barest of economic reasons: to avoid if at all possible the adverse economic impact that such embarrassing revelations would bring to the city. I submit that the same method of denial employed to stonewall information about human rights and civil rights violations was used to stonewall the Denton Connection to President Kennedy's assassination. Such denial permeates the several Denton sub-connections presented below.

Rightist/Neo-Nazi Connections

Bradford Angers, a former military analyst and private investigator, worked briefly for H.L. Hunt in 1963 before resigning his post due to a disagreement with Hunt over his assignments. In a story told to Dick Russell, Angers places Larrie Schmidt in Denton County several weeks after the assassination under suspicious circumstances. Schmidt and his wife apparently were beaten up and thrown out of a car, and a Denton County Deputy Sheriff stopped to assist them. Schmidt gave the Deputy a false I.D., which may have prevented the story from appearing in the Denton paper.[16]

Schmidt, of course, was the leader of a small group known as Conservatism-USA that hoped to infiltrate a large number of ultra-right organizations and take them over. CUSA would then become a major force in American politics; in Schmidt's most grandiose thoughts, a ruling party. He and his brother got quite close to the Edwin Walker entourage in Dallas before the General discovered that the Schmidts had designs on his organization. The Schmidts were cast out of Walker's group and bitterly condemned by all close to the General.[17]

Suspects in the assault on Schmidt were plentiful in Denton. You might say there were 28 of them in the Young Republicans Club of North Texas, a campus organization at North Texas State University.[18] Walker's ideas were very popular among the rank and file of this group as well as its leadership. According to a November 4, 1963 Criminal Intelligence Report by Dallas Police Department detectives Jack Revill and H.M. Hart, four Young Republicans – William Drew Fitz, Ronnie Beall, M.R. Bowlin and William Ivan Snodgrass – visited General Walker's home. Later, they joined 15-25 more NTSU students at the U.S. Day rally on October 23, 1963.[19] This Walker-sponsored event was the day before Adlai Stevenson's visit to Dallas and is viewed as the event that set the stage for the ugly incident the following night in which Stevenson was spat upon and hit with a placard. NTSU students – about 20 of them – participated in the Stevenson protest on October 24 and it was former student Robert Hatfield who spat upon Stevenson and was arrested for aggravated assault and inciting a riot.[20] The *Dallas Morning News* reported on October 25 that an NTSU student assaulted the Ambassador, but the reference to the school was dropped in later editions after the Registrar confirmed that Hatfield was not currently enrolled. However, Hatfield did have friends at the school who were enrolled in the fall of 1963 and who identified themselves as members of the John Birch Society.[21]

The venom displayed by the North Texas youngsters against the U.N., and against Stevenson, was just a warm up, they said, for President Kennedy's visit the following month. Long and ugly demonstrations were in the works. William Fitz, one of the youngsters who met Walker before the U.S. Day rally, had this charming remark about JFK's upcoming visit: "we will drag his dick in the dirt."[22] The demonstrations, after a visit from the FBI, never materialized. As Professor Jerry Rose observed in 1989, perhaps the group had other plans.[23]

Fitz appears on page 234 of the 1963 *The Yucca*, the student yearbook of NTSU, along with the 27 other Young Republicans. As appropriate given the drab conformity of the era, he is conservatively dressed in a dark plaid suit and narrow tie, much like the other male students who belonged to student organizations and who dutifully lined up for yearbook pictures. He looks no different, really than any of the Tri-Betas who appear on the pages before, or the Young Democrats or West Dormers who appear on the pages afterward.[24] And his organization, despite the word that must have spread on the small campus indicating YRC involvement in the Walker rally and the Stevenson protests, continued to enjoy the full support of the university administration. Not a single Young Republican, as far as I can tell, was ever censured or investigated or expelled for his or her role in the Stevenson incident or the raucous rally the evening before.[25]

The city's newspapers showed no investigatory interest in these unbecoming episodes. The NTSU campus paper *Campus Chat* editorialized that Robert Hatfield was a former student who was placed on probation for poor grades in 1961 and was satisfied that this fact absolved the university administration or the student body of any responsibility for the Dallas embarrassments.[26] Across town at the *Record-Chronicle*, editors were in full cover-up mode on Hatfield. The paper reported on page two only that he was an Irving resident who was not enrolled at NTSU.[27] Going unreported was his accrual of enough semester hours at North Texas State to be classified as a sophomore by the fall of 1961, and his ongoing friendships with campus Birchists during the fall of 1963.[28] The paper's stonewalling could be read as a backhanded congratulation to Hatfield for what he did to wreck Stevenson's visit. Only days before the Ambassador came to Dallas the paper editorialized against any show of celebration for the U.N., using arguments that John Birch himself would have appreciated: "This is the week to salute the United Nations but a lot of facts make you wonder whether we should salute or merely give up."[29]

In the aftermath of the most regrettable public relations fiasco in school history, the Young Republicans continued as if nothing untoward had happened. The group continued to host distinguished speakers such as Evelyn Huey[30] (earlier in the fall, they welcomed

George H.W. Bush, then a rising star in Houston[31]) and at the first spring meeting of 1964, the growing organization hosted *Record-Chronicle* editor Tom Kirkland, whose paper, as we've seen was in complete denial on the Hatfield-Birchist-Young Republican connections.[32]

One is also struck, looking at the yearbook photo once again, at the relatively small size of the Young Republicans Club. There were only 28 members pictured, and a few more did not show for the picture. This means that if 20 to 30 of them appeared at the U.S. Day rally, and 20 or so appeared at the Stevenson demonstration, as Revill and Hart's sources implied,[33] then this would have been a significant portion, nearly all, of the Young Republican organization, even taking into account that some of the protestors, like Robert Hatfield, were officially former students, and some others may have been provocateurs, informants, wannabes and hangers-on who were not really part of the group. A "Walker movement" at NTSU, then would not have been some deviant subculture or splinter group within the YRC but would have had the sympathy, if not the support of the majority of the Young Republicans at the University. Indeed, Confidential Informant T-1 acknowledged to Revill and Hart that a Walker movement was underway at the school, and the prominent figures in that group were also prominent in the YRC. The leader of the Walker movement, Les Tooker, claimed to be a YRC officer, while another Walkerite, Bill Snodgrass, was the YRC's treasurer and representative on the organization's State Executive Board for two years.[34]

The appalling lack of concern exhibited by the university and the city about the exploits of Hatfield and the others in the October incidents in Dallas must be considered in the context of the Birchist slant of the city in general. That extreme conservatism is evident in several ways. Even before Kennedy was elected a group called Students for Religious Freedom flooded campus mailboxes with anti-Catholic literature which argued that a Roman Catholic is ineligible to be president.[35] Then, we encountered (as already mentioned) the

Birchist language of the editorials in the local daily, and such language also found its way into *Campus Chat*. Two student editorialists took a firm stand against President Kennedy's civil rights bill because it dictated to businessmen who they could serve at their establishments[36] and another student questioned the legality of Israel's tactics in capturing Third Reich criminal Adolph Eichmann.[37] Not wanting to be left out of the fun, Walkerites Fitz and Snodgrass weighed in with letters to the editor. Fitz argued that *Campus Chat* was not far enough to the Right to suit him, comparing it to Communist publications.[38] Snodgrass trumpeted the conservative cause, asking questions reminiscent of the infamous November 22 black-bordered ad: "Why ... should we subsidize the Communists and their allies? Will they love us for it? Why should we negotiate with Communists? Why should we not use force on the Communists?"[39]

The choice of speakers invited to campus during 1962 and 1963 also displayed a distinct rightward, even extremist, tilt. Fred Schwarz, President of the Christian Anti-Communist Crusade, appeared before the

Baptist Student Union on March 20, 1962.[40] Schwarz put on "schools" for anti-Communists that so alarmed Arnold Forster and Benjamin Epstein that the veteran extremist watchers devoted a chapter to them in their book, *Danger on the Right*.[41] Then, in 1963, representatives of the United States Information Agency (USIA) appeared March 22.[42] The USIA is best known for its activities in the McCarthy era, and though headed by Edward Morrow in 1963, still harbored what Dr. Rose called a "Loyal American Underground:" civil servants beholden to no particular administration, and a hangover from the McCarthy era that was overly preoccupied with Communist conspiracies.[43] That preoccupation was still very much alive in the early Sixties: the agency translated one of Fred Schwarz' books, *You Can Trust the Communists*, and assisted with its distribution overseas.[44] The USIA considered North Texas State a friendly audience for its propaganda and even picked some NTSU students to appear in one of its films, the purpose of which was to project a clean, wholesome image of American students to the world community.[45]

The city's conservatism and that of the university was also evident in the lack of seriousness and concern generated by several waves of neo-Nazi activity that hit Denton in May and June 1963. The Young Republicans should have been prime suspects in these outbreaks but were not even questioned by the police. On May 1, to protest a speech given on campus by a Houston Anti-Defamation League representative, American Nazi Party leaflets were distributed along city streets and in the parking lot of a Sears Roebuck store. The same day, several Nazis were seen marching in the 500 block of Sycamore St. near the NTSU campus.[46] The *Record-Chronicle* flatly denied that Dentonites could have been involved, saying instead that "visitors" to the city were to blame, citing the misspellings on the leaflets and the fact that the swastikas were printed incorrectly.[47] (The swastikas were printed inside out, and the *Record-Chronicle* implied that Denton Nazis would have been much smarter than this. I think it was the work of very smart students, trying to outfox the police.) An ANP leader in Sacramento later wrote to the paper to inform editor Kirkland that the Nazis were, in fact locals,[48] and that more action was forthcoming. But Kirkland treated it all as a big joke: "Better dust off that gas mask boys, we're in for some more activity any day now."[49]

The Sacramento ANP leader turned out to be right. Four more outbursts of neo-Nazi activity occurred in Denton before the end of June.[50] In total, there were 13 separate incidents in the May-June period, all but two happening within one mile of the campus, in the "college town" section of the city.[51] As early as May 23, Denton police chief Andy Anderson shrugged off the incidents, attributing them to "juveniles,"[52] this despite a *Campus Chat* report that two men in their early twenties were involved.[53]

Dealey Plaza Connections

Of all the Denton connections, the most significant one may be the possibility that a Young Republican was stationed behind the stockade fence, assisting in a conspiracy. Lee

Bower's description of a man "... about mid-twenties, in either a plaid shirt or plaid coat or jacket ..."[54] would have fit any of the older Young Republican males and one Walkerite in particular: Bill Snodgrass, 23 years old.[55] Snodgrass, a YRC officer, we've already met.

Bowers' description also fits 23-year-old Larry H. Florer, a 1962 NTSU graduate with a degree in accounting. Not only was Florer in Dealey Plaza – wearing a plaid suit coat – but he acted suspiciously enough to be taken into custody for questioning about the assassination.[56] Florer's deposition to the Sheriff's Department stated that he watched the motorcade on Poydras Street with a friend, then retreated to a barbecue joint on Pacific Avenue for lunch. After hearing of the shooting, he apparently abandoned his friend, who needed to return to work, and walked along Pacific until he encountered the confused scene in Dealey Plaza. He then entered the third floor of the Records Building to use a phone, and finding none available, returned to the street. His actions lead several witnesses to say that he was drunk, although he was not arrested for public intoxication after talking to officers, and was released after questioning.[57]

About 250 feet from the spot where Florer was whisked away to the Sheriff's office, former Dentonites Maggie Brown and Aurelia Alonzo had gathered at 12:30 to cheer on the President's motorcade and to get a glimpse of what Jackie was wearing. Brown was a 1963 NTSU journalism graduate who was employed as a women's page copy editor at the *Dallas Morning News*.[58] She found a spot on the north side of Elm, near a freeway sign, alongside three *DMN* colleagues: former NTSU journalism pal Alonzo, Ann Donaldson, and Mary Woodward.[59] Woodward, of course, would figure prominently in a famous controversy after the assassination. She was the reporter who was quite upset by what she saw and rushed back to the *News* to write a story. The story stated that the shots came from the area of the grassy knoll.[60]

Brown and Alonzo come off badly in the aftermath of the assassination if the account of Hugh Aynesworth is to be believed. Aynesworth, a respected Dallas journalist, wrote that Brown, Alonzo, and Donaldson all rushed to Woodward after an early edition of her story was published, and attempted to talk Woodward out of her assertion that shots originated from the knoll.[61]

Brown was a dedicated career woman at North Texas State who gradually worked her way up the ranks of the student journalism organizations and the *Campus Chat* staff.[62] Her chum Alonzo (whose last name has been misspelled in the assassination literature as "Lorenzo"[63]) was a "Big Woman on Campus" type who took Denton by storm before leaving to work at the *Morning News*. After the pretty freshman made a "big splash" working at *Campus Chat* in 1959 and on *The Yucca* in 1960, she went on to star in several campus clubs and capped off a whirlwind junior year as editor of *The Yucca* for 1961.[64] Both women, then, were clearly part of the campus establishment. That these establishment types would support the official version of "three shots from the TSBD" is not surprising, and even expected, given what we know of the campus and the city.[65] The conservatism of Denton and NTSU was not the only reason for the reaction of the women to the assassination, of course, but I believe unequivocally that it helped to shape or condition that reaction.

Dentonite Jim Featherston was known to Brown and Alonzo as a respected competitor at the *Dallas Times-Herald*. He was stationed at the corner of Main and Houston so that he could retrieve a roll of film from Bob Jackson, an *Associated Press* photographer who was in a press truck several cars in back of the President's limousine. Shortly after he retrieved the film, he heard several reports that he did not immediately distinguish as gun shots. Asking a colleague what had happened, he was pointed in the direction of Mary Moorman and Jean Hill on the south side of Elm, and Featherston will be long remembered as the reporter who gathered up the Moorman photograph, and as the first interviewer of both Moorman and Hill.[66]

Despite his journalistic coup, Featherston, like Brown and Alonzo, made a poor impression on researchers. According to Richard Trask, Featherston browbeat the two young witnesses into an interview and held them "captive" in a press room until sometime after 6:00 P.M.[67] He is accused, furthermore, of stealing Moorman's photo and allowing it to be missing at several junctures during the afternoon of the 22nd.[68] Finally, he has been criticized for instructing Jean Hill not to report her citing of a man running west into the Depository parking lot immediately after the assassination.[69]

After The Assassination

The first physician to reach Trauma Room One and to begin treating President Kennedy at Parkland Hospital, according to most accounts, was surgical intern Dr. Charles J. Carrico, a 1957 NTSU grad who went on to distinguish himself in the early Sixties as a star medical student at the University of Texas Southwestern Medical School.[70] Carrico's story of a small, round, "penetrating" hole in the President's throat, which he subsequently changed in testimony before the Warren Commission,[71] has long been cited as evidence that the throat wound was one of entry rather than exit. His early testimony on the head wound[72] which he later told Gerald Posner was in error,[73] also supported a frontal shot. The fact that Carrico changed his mind about his testimony and did not speak up sooner about controversial aspects of it[74] is very much in keeping with the others who make up the Denton Connection. The "official" version of events was sacrosanct, and not to be tampered with.[75]

While Dr. Carrico struggled in vain to save the President, and while Brown, Alonzo and Featherston were coping with the reality of what they had just seen and the Dealey Plaza mayhem that followed, Bill Moyers was just learning that the President had been shot.[76] He was lunching in Austin, where he had been assigned the task of advance man for the Kennedy entourage that was to appear in the city that evening. Recovering from his initial shock, Moyers managed to hitch a ride on a private plane and boarded *Air Force One* at Love Field less than two hours later. Johnson needed a Kennedy insider, one that he knew well, to help smooth over the presidential transition period, and Moyers, 29 years old at the time, fit the bill perfectly.[77]

Johnson and Moyers were old friends. Then-Senator Johnson, a conservative Democrat, received a letter from then-East Texas schoolboy Moyers and was immediately impressed. It would be a while before Moyers joined Johnson's staff as a summer intern, however. First, Moyers needed to cut his teeth in politics and did so in Denton, where he followed a family tradition by attending NTSU.[78] Moyers was an absolute smash at North Texas State, being elected President of his class and Outstanding Student in his Freshman and Sophomore years. At LBJ's request, Moyers transferred to the University of Texas in Austin to finish his undergraduate education. He then worked on a divinity degree at Southwestern Baptist Theological Seminary and was about to settle into a teaching job at Baylor University when he was tapped to serve on Johnson's staff, and later, rose to be Deputy Director of the Peace Corps under President Kennedy.[79]

Campus Chat bragged that Moyers was a close advisor to Johnson in the early hours of the new administration[80] and indeed Moyers did appear to be everywhere at once in the critical hours and days after the tragedy in Dallas.[81] A critical link in Johnson's impromptu transition team, he was in the thick of discussions about what kind of investigation to proceed with in the midst of rumors that several independent investigations were being planned and that Russia or Cuba might be blamed for Kennedy's death if such investigations ran their course. As we now know, the intra-governmental discussions were leading toward a controlled and limited inquiry. First, there was the idea of a Texas inquiry which would have emerged without independent scrutiny beyond Texas officials and the FBI, an idea the Washington elite nixed. Then, Nicolas deB. Katzenbach wrote to Moyers on the 25th that he believed that an FBI report should be released as soon as possible to convince the public that Oswald was the assassin and that he had no confederates who were still at large.[82] We could hardly put the full blame on Moyers, not yet 30 years old, for the entire Warren Commission mess that followed. It is evident, though, that Moyers did little at a key point in history to discourage the idea of a presidential

Commission, one that would be a whitewash from the start, one created to establish what Epstein called "political truth,"[83] but not the facts, in the JFK case. Denton denies or fails to consider that Moyers may have done the country a disservice in the early hours of the Johnson Administration, and continues to welcome him back to campus as a distinguished alum and conquering hero.[84]

Not long after Moyers left NTSU, Mike Howard began his studies in Government on the Denton campus.[85] After graduating in 1958, he joined the U.S. Secret Service as an agent.[86] He spent several days after the assassination with the Oswald family and was later given the task of guarding Lynda Bird Johnson.[87] Howard was given high marks by Robert Oswald for the compassion he displayed to the entire Oswald family,[88] but his actions have been scrutinized carefully by Dick Russell and Peter Dale Scott. Russell was suspicious of Howard's post-assassination assignments, wanting to know why Howard spent so much time with Peter Gregory, Marguerite Oswald, and Marina Oswald on the day of Lee Oswald's death. Scott answered that Howard used his Great

Southwest Corporation contacts to place Marina Oswald in *The Inn at Six Flags*, and did so even before he was authorized to do so by President Johnson.[89] Much more information about Howard needs to be gathered, and he remains one of the most controversial and least understood Denton connections.

Denton Today

The covering up of the city's links to the assassination is one of many factors that contributed to Denton's growth since the Sixties. By 1996, with the city untarnished by the killing of the President, the unrestrained civic boosterism of Denton's business elite had finally yielded some dividends. By that date, the city shared, occasionally, joint economic billing with Dallas and Fort Worth – the Dallas-Fort Worth-Denton region being referred to in selected advertisements as the "Metroplex Triangle."[90]

Economic progress did not mean that Denton now takes a lighter view of the assassination. Today Denton is as vigilant as ever about stonewalling and denying its connections to the event. While the City of Dallas was able to turn Dealey Plaza into North Texas' number one tourist attraction, no such plans are in the works in Denton for Robert Oswald's former home at 1009 Sierra, or Room 154 of the Business Administration Building, the meeting place of the Young Republicans Club. Painful and embarrassing reminders of the city's links to the assassination continue to be unwelcome here, for the same reason, I think as always: they would be bad for Denton's image and its businesses.[91]

Denton prospered in the aftermath of the assassination, and so did the Denton Connection. Moyers, Carrico, and M.R. Bowlin all received Distinguished Alumnus Awards from NTSU (now known as the University of North Texas.)[92] Bowlin, of Pacific Palisades, California, who broke bread with General Walker and roomed with the charming William Fitz in 1963,[93] is the retired Chairman and CEO of Atlantic Richfield Company.[94] Because of his successful career, he takes his place alongside other big name alums and friends who are campus legends, including (in addition to Carrico and Moyers) Gene Autry, Ross Perot, Phyllis George, Larry McMurty, Lucille Murchison, Eddie Chiles, Pat Boone, Roy Orbison, Don Henley, Paul Shaffer, Joe Greene, Don January, and more recently, Dr. Phil McGraw and Norah Jones.[95] In 1996, the alumni newspaper *North Texan* listed Bowlin as a "President's Fellow" for his large financial contributions to the university.[96]

Closing Comments

We have seen how the extremely conservative political ideology that consumed NTSU and Denton may have had a profound effect on the events of November 22, 1963. The White Alliance in particular drew strength from this ideology, and the town's sympathy with that set of ideas meant that the Birchist students were never, as far as I can tell, officially reprimanded for their deplorable conduct, or censured or probated in any way for it. This ideology was also strongly pro-business, consequently, the numerous embarrassing linkages between

Denton and the assassination have been stonewalled and covered up. This has been done for the barest of economic reasons: to avoid the adverse economic impact that such revelations would have produced.

The conservatism of Denton, led, additionally, to the acceptance among the Denton Connection of "officially constructed" knowledge, and denial or repudiation of all other knowledge. Key Dentonites observed the assassination and dealt with its aftermath. What they reported or constructed, and what they did, more often than not was in line with the city's conservatism. This information and action, taken as a whole, functioned to keep a lid on relevant evidence that, had it been examined carefully in the months and years soon after the event, could have led to prosecution of the individuals responsible for the assassination. I submit that the ideology prevalent in the city provided a social milieu that spawned several assassination-related denials: the university and city ignored and essentially denied the radicalism of the Birchist students; Brown and Alonzo denied that shots came from the front of the motorcade; Carrico failed to confirm that the President throat wound was one of entry; and Moyers contributed to the developing "official" denial, as early as November 22, that someone other than Oswald was involved in the assassination.

We have also uncovered a most unusual brand of assassination suspect. In the past we have looked upon suspects as swarthy underworld types who killed the President for a price, never really knowing who was running them or why. These murky people lived in the subterranean underbelly of what Peter Dale Scott called a "Gray Alliance" of underworld types who had tie-ins to upper-world counterparts in legitimate society.[97] In Denton, we found a "White Alliance" – fully legitimated young rightists and Birchists whose possible involvement in the assassination may have been brashly stonewalled for the barest of local economic reasons. Dr. Scott's Gray Alliance stretched from the netherworld all the way to J. Edgar Hoover. We need more research to determine whether Denton's White Alliance was just a local outbreak of youthful racist radicalism or something that was connected to higher-ups in governmental or corporate institutions. John Dabney Murchison's widow, Lucille Murchison is on the Board of Regents of the University of North Texas.[98] The relationships that may have existed between the Murchison family (and Great Southwest), Mike Howard, Bill Moyers, Larry Florer and the White Alliance are among the more important Denton connections that remain to be explored.

ENDNOTES

[1] Robert Oswald, *Lee: A Portrait of Lee Harvey Oswald by His Brother*. New York: Coward-McCann, Inc., 1967, pp. 11-28, 135-182.

[2] "Denton Man is Brother of Suspect," *Denton Record-Chronicle*, November 24, 1963, Section 4, p. 7.

[3] *Ibid.*

[4] Robert Oswald, *ibid*, p. 171.

[5] To finish up Bob Oswald: he was so afraid of backlash from Dentonites that he decided to leave Marina and her two children in the care of James Martin, a decision he later regretted. Following Martin's first appearance before the Warren Commission, Secret Service protection of Marina and family was dropped and Robert immediately invited Marina, June, and Rachel to live with him in Denton. Marina and June did live in Denton at 1009 Sierra, but only for about a week (Rachel stayed with the Martins.) Not long after departing from there, Marina bought a home in Richardson, Texas. See Oswald, *ibid*; Gerald Ford and John Stiles, *Portrait of the Assassin.* New York: Simon and Schuster, 1965, pp. 348, 353, 457, 464; Priscilla McMillan, *Marina and Lee.* New York: Harper and Row (Book Club Edition), 1977, p. 561.

Researchers should also be aware that there was another Robert Oswald in Denton in 1963. Robert M. Oswald received his B.A. degree in Psychology at North Texas State that year and was listed in the 1962 student directory as a commuting student who lived in Richardson (so was Ona Jolene Oswald, relationship to Robert M. Oswald unknown.) This second Robert Oswald now resides in Fairhope, Alabama. See *North Texas State University Student Directory*, Fall, 1962, p. 135; *University of North Texas Alumni Directory*, 1994, p. 441.

[6] Jerry Rose, "J.B. Stoner: An Introduction," *Fourth Decade*, Volume 3, Number 1, November 1995, pp. 25-29; "Oswald and the Nazis," *Fourth Decade*, Volume 3, Number 2, January 1996, pp. 21-25.

[7] *Dynamic Denton*, sound recording produced by Norsworthy-Mercer, Inc. for the City of Denton, 1967.

[8] *Denton City Directory*, 1961, p. 10.

[9] *Ibid*; see also *Texas Realtor*, April 1971, p. 32.

[10] C.A. Bridges, *History of Denton, Texas*. Waco: Texian Press, 1978, pp. 433-470; "The

New Denton," *Denton Record-Chronicle*, June 4, 1963, p. 4.

[11] Jane Wolfe, *The Murchisons*. New York: St. Martin's Paperbacks, 1991, p. 296.

[12] C. Wright Mills in *The Power Elite* (New York: Oxford University Press, 1956, Chapter Two) documents how a quiet informality dominated the decision making of local elites of the era. The elite families of Denton appear regularly in the official histories of the town: see for instance Bridges, *ibid.*

[13] James Marlow, "Part of JFK's Civil Rights Program Faces Tough Battle," *Denton Record-Chronicle*, June 25, 1963, p. 4; William Theis, "Lawmakers Balk on Rights Move," *Dallas Morning News*, June 20, 1963, p. 1; "Civil Rights," *Dallas Morning News*, June 21, 1963, Section 4, p. 2; Duff Daniels, "Civil Rights Bill Puts Liberty in Jeopardy," *Campus Chat* (student newspaper of North Texas State University), June 28, 1963, p. 2; Tom Boone, "Section of Rights Bill Hurts

Free Enterprise," *Campus Chat*, March 25, 1964, p. 2.

[14] Extremist watchers at the Anti-Defamation League and the Southern Poverty Law Center, among others, have adequately written this history. The ADL documented 630 violent incidents (e.g., floggings, stabbings, arson, bombings) against the civil rights movement in the South between 1962 and 1966 and an additional 422 anti-Semitic incidents such as cemetery desecrations, vandalism against synagogues, arson, and shootings. See "Enact Gun Laws Now For Safety," *The Dixon Line*, Volume 4, Number 4, February 1967, p. 1.

[15] This violent underside of the history of Denton and other Southern towns goes unreported in the official records, and is mostly undocumented except for the efforts of extremist watchers and a few social scientists. For Denton's traditional or "official" history, see Ed Bates, *History and Reminiscences of Denton County*. Denton: Terrill Wheeler, 1989; Bridges, 1978; Denton

Centennial Commission, *Centurama*. Denton, Texas, 1957; *The Denton Review*, published quarterly by the Historical Society of Denton County; Bullitt Lowry, *Historical Markers of Denton County, Texas*. Denton: Denton County Historical Commission, 1980; Edwin Odom and Bullitt Lowry, *A Brief History of Denton County, Texas*. Denton: Terrill Wheeler, 1975; Gayle Strages, *Portraits of Denton*. Austin: Nortex Press, 1986; *Handbook of Northern Texas*. Chicago: C.S. Burch, 1886; *Denton, Texas: The City of Homes, Schools, and Colleges*. Denton: Chamber of Commerce, no date; Emily Fowler and Alma Chambers, *Towns and Communities of Denton County, Texas*. Emily Fowler Public Library, Denton, no date. For a sampling of the social science literature, see Stewart Tolnay and E.M. Beck, "Lethal Social Control in the South: Lynchings and Executions Between 1880 and 1930." Pp. 176-195 in George S. Bridges and Martha A. Myers, (Eds), *Inequality, Crime, and Social Control*. Boulder: Westview Press, 1994; James Marquart, Sheldon Ekland-Olson and Jonathan R. Sorensen, *The Rope,*

The Chair and the Needle: Capital Punishment in Texas, 1923-1990. Austin: University of Texas Press, 1994; M. Watt Espy, *Executions in the United States, 1608-1991.* Ann Arbor: Inter-University Consortium for Political and Social Research, 1992.

[16] Dick Russell, *The Man Who Knew Too Much.* New York: Carroll and Graf, 1992, pp. 325-326. "Hard luck" stories along Stemmons (such as the misfortune that the Schmidts encountered) usually made the local paper because of their human interest value and also to remind the locals that bad things can happen in the rapidly growing city if you hang out along the highway. The assault described by Angers is perfect fodder for such a local story, but I could find no reference to it in the Denton paper. Persons suffering from hard luck were routinely identified in such news stories, and the Sheriff's inability to positively identify the Schmidts may have kept their particular story out of the paper.

[17] Russell, *ibid*, pp. 320-327; Jerry Rose, "Nut Country: The Friends of General Walker," *Third Decade*, Volume 5, Number 5, July 1989, pp. 12-17; Pat Swank, "A Plot That Flopped," *Look*, January 26, 1965, pp. 28-29.

[18] *The Yucca* (student yearbook of North Texas State University), 1963, p. 234. Twenty-eight are pictured here, and there were some no-shows. There was no listing of the Young Republicans who failed to show up for the photo session.

[19] Memo of Jack Revill and H.M. Hart to W.P. Ganaway regarding Political Demonstrations, November 5, 1963. Document provided courtesy of Jerry Rose.

[20] Mike Quinn, "Stevenson Struck With Sign, Booed," *Dallas Morning News*, October 25, 1963, p. 1; *Campus Chat*, November 1, 1963, p. 2; "Stevenson Banged Up After Dallas Speech, *Denton Record-Chronicle*, October 25, 1963, p. 1.

[21] Keith Shelton, "Stevenson Voices Shock Over Near-Riot After Talk," *Dallas Times-Herald*, October 25, 1963, p. 13.

[22] Memo of Revill and Hart to Ganaway, November 5, 1963; Commission Exhibit 710, "Memo of Jack Revill to W.P. Ganaway Regarding Criminal Intelligence Section Preparation for the Visit of John F. Kennedy to Dallas on November 22, 1963," *Fourth Decade*, Volume 3, Number 3, March, 1996, back cover.

[23] Rose, *ibid*, p. 13.

[24] *The Yucca*, 1963, pp. 222-235.

[25] *Campus Chat*, issues of October 25, 30, and November 1; *Denton Record-Chronicle*, issues of October 25-31. The names of any students disciplined would not have been released to the public per university policy. However, the fact that certain students had been disciplined, or were going to be disciplined, would have been reported in the student newspaper or the *Record-Chronicle*.

Searching both sources, I could find no evidence of any official disciplinary action against any of the protesting students.

[26] Bill Perkins, "Press Gives NTSU Unearned Black Eye," *Campus Chat*, November 1, 1963, p. 2.

[27] *Denton Record-Chronicle*, October 25, 1963, p. 2.

[28] *North Texas State University Student Directory*, Fall, 1961, p. 59; Shelton, ibid.

[29] "Little Reason For Joy," *Denton Record-Chronicle*, October 22, 1963, p. 4.

[30] Evelyn Huey was one of the first women to teach at NTSU. See "Dr. Huey To Speak on Election Reform," *Campus Chat*, November 1, 1963.

[31] Republican Calls For Unity of Party," *Campus Chat*, October 18, 1963, p. 1.

[32] *The Yucca*, 1964, p. 178.

[33] Memo of Revill and Hart to Ganaway, November 5, 1963.

[34] *Ibid*; "Young Republicans Elect Four to Executive Board," *Campus Chat*, October 7, 1960, p. 3; "YR Delegates Represent NT at Convention," *Campus Chat*, March 16, 1962, p. 6.

[35] "Anti-Catholic Mail Floods P.O. Boxes," *Campus Chat*, October 26, 1960, p. 1.

[36] Daniels, *ibid*; Boone, *ibid*.

[37] Phil Vinson, "Eichmann Case Over?" *Campus Chat*, June 22, 1962.

[38] Chat Found Comparable to USSR Publications, *Campus Chat*, March 20, 1964, p. 2.

[39] "White House Needs Conservative," *Campus Chat*, March 13, 1964.

[40] "Baptists Study Communism, Discuss 'God vs. Anti-God,'" *Campus Chat*, March 16, 1962.

[41] Arnold Forster and Benjamin Epstein, *Danger on the Right*. New York: Random House, 1964, pp. 47-67.

[42] "USIA, Peace Corps Deputies To Address Journalism Parley," *Campus Chat*, March 13, 1963, p. 1.

[43] Jerry Rose, "The Loyal American Underground," *Fourth Decade*, Volume 1, Number 5, July 1994, pp. 28-31.

[44] Forster and Epstein, *ibid*, p. 44.

[45] Karen Goodmon, "U.S. Information Agency Shoots Film of Graduate Music Student," *Campus Chat*, March 1, 1963, p. 1.

[46] "Nazi Cards Are Left In City," *Denton Record-Chronicle*, May 2, 1963, p. 1.

[47] *Ibid*.

[48] "Denton Nazis Should Have Swastikas Right Next Time," *Denton Record-Chronicle*, May 20, 1963.

[49] *Ibid.*

[50] "Juveniles Believed Responsible For Denton Swastikas," *Denton Record-Chronicle*, May 24, 1963, p. 1; "Paint Remover In Order As Swastikas Appear In City," *Denton Record-Chronicle*, June 2, 1963, p. 2; "Police Checking Clothing Thefts, City Vandalism," *Denton Record-Chronicle*, June 24, 1963, p. 2.

[51] The targets were as follows. May 1 (index cards with swastikas): St. Andrew Presbyterian Church, Sears Roebuck between Oak and Hickory, *Record-Chronicle* building at 314 E. Hickory. May 1 (marching): 500 Sycamore. May 19 (black swastika painted on house): 1225 W. Oak. May 23 (index card): 314 E. Hickory. May 23 (swastika poster): 1225 W. Oak. May 31 (red spray painted swastikas): city jail-police building, 314 E.

Hickory, 111 W. University, 315 S. Locust, 906 W. Center. The two incidents that were more than a mile from campus were not far away either, both being within 1.3 miles of the campus.

[52] *Denton Record-Chronicle*, May 24, 1963, p. 1.

[53] Dick Beane, "Nazis Could Arouse Appreciation of U.S.," *Campus Chat*, June 7, 1963, p. 2.

[54] Jim Marrs, *Crossfire*. New York: Carroll and Graf, 1989, p. 76.

[55] *The Yucca*, 1964, pp. 178, 386.

[56] Richard Trask, *Pictures of the Pain*. Danvers: Yeoman Press, 1994, pp. 163, 547-548.

[57] *Ibid*, pp. 547-548.

[58] Peter Whitmey, "Mary E. Woodward: The First Dissenting Witness," *Third Decade*,

Volume 8, Number 5, July 1992, pp. 24-26; "Some Questions," *Texas Observer*, December 13, 1963, p. 9.

[59] Mary Woodward, "Witness From The News Describes Assassination," *Dallas Morning News*, November 23, 1963, p. 3.

[60] Whitmey, *ibid*, p. 24.

[61] *Ibid*, p. 26.

[62] *The Yucca*: 1960, p. 334; 1961, p. 449; 1962, p. 114; 1963, pp. 187, 215. *Campus Chat*: February 24, 1961, p. 2; September 22, 1961, p. 6; January 5, 1962, p. 2; February 1, 1963, p. 2.

[63] Anthony Summers, *Conspiracy*. New York: Paragon House, 1989, p. 27; Bobby Dodds, *The Kennedy Chronicle*, 1994, p. 27; Whitmey, p, 24.

[64] *The Yucca*: 1960, pp. 92, 331; 1961, pp. 110, 114, 118, 244-245, 260. *Campus Chat*: September 18, 1959, p. 2; June 10, 1960, p. 2.

[65] The official view at the *News* was apparently a wedding of early wire service reports of three shots being fired at the motorcade, and Kent Biffle's piece "Assassin Crouched and Took Deadly Aim." See *Dallas Morning News*, November 23, 1963, Section 1, p. 1 and Section 4, p. 1.

[66] Trask, pp. 236-242. Featherston lived at 1010 Edinburg in Denton and made the daily commute to Dallas to work at the *Times-Herald*.

[67] *Ibid.*

[68] *Ibid*; Darwin Payne, *The Press Corps and the Kennedy Assassination*. Lexington, KY: Association for Education in Journalism, 1970, p. 26; Bill Sloan, *JFK: The Last Dissenting Witness*. Gretna: Pelican Publishing Company, 1992, p. 32. Featherston gets a more sympathetic review from former *Times-Herald* colleague Connie Kritzberg in *Secrets From The Sixth Floor* (Tulsa, OK: Under Cover Press, 1994.) For a

balanced and fair account of Featherston (and Aynesworth) see Sheldon Inkol, "Reporters Remember 11-22-63," *Fourth Decade*, Volume 1, Number 2, January 1994, pp. 28-31.

[69] Trask, *ibid.* Another journalistic effort of note that upholds the official account and tries to uplift the sagging morale of the Dallas police is Judy Bonner's *Investigation of a Homicide* (Anderson, SC: Droke House, 1969). Bonner is a 1953 graduate of Texas State College for Women (now Texas Woman's University), the "second" school in Denton, located about a mile from North Texas State.

It is only fair to point out that not all of the Denton Connections are negative. Not far from Featherston, on the south side of Elm near the intersection of Elm and Houston, was a 1948 NTSU grad, Phil Willis. Willis shot twenty-seven pictures that have been a most valuable resource for researchers over the years, particularly during the hotly debated "Black Dog Man" controversy. Not cowed by the official version of events in

Dealey Plaza, Willis maintained that at least one shot was fired from the grassy knoll, and he even volunteered a lead for researchers to follow concerning the possibly fake epileptic attack that occurred in the Plaza only moments before the President's motorcade arrived.

Three writers who studied at NTSU– Jim Marrs, Jens Hansen and Coke Buchanan – have contributed to accounts that dispute the official version; Marrs' book *Crossfire* became one of the main works consulted by Oliver Stone in the research leading up to his movie, *JFK*. In addition, former NTSU graduate student William Allen shot the controversial *Times-Herald* photo on the south side of Elm of Buddy Walthers, patrolman J.W. Foster and the FBI mystery man believed to be Robert Barrett; and former *Campus Chat* editor Jimmy Darnell was the young reporter who secured one of the first live television interviews of Jean Hill. See Trask, p. 543; Charles Crenshaw with Jens Hansen and J. Gary Shaw, *JFK Conspiracy of Silence*. New York: Penguin Group, 1992; Beverly Oliver with Coke

Buchanan, *Nightmare in Dallas*. Lancaster, PA: Starburst Publishers, 1994; Mark Oakes, *Eyewitness Video, Part II.* Irving TX, 1994; Sloan, pp. 30-32.

[70] *North Texan* (alumni newspaper of NTSU), October, 1961, p. 3.

[71] *The Witnesses*. New York: McGraw-Hill, 1965, pp. 83-93.

[72] *Ibid.*

[73] Gerald Posner, *Case Closed.* New York: Random House, 1993, p. 311.

[74] Dr. Carrico allowed himself to be led by Arlen Specter in his testimony before the Warren Commission. Specter essentially put words in Carrico's mouth. Had Dr. Carrico kept to his original story, the Warren Commission's conclusions might have been different. His further testimony that he could see the throat wound before nurses took off the President's clothes (it was above the knot of the President's tie) is an additional and

significant rebuttal of the single bullet theory. However, the Commission ignored the testimony and Carrico failed to raise the issue with researchers after appearing before the Commission. To make matters worse, the information that he has provided to researchers has sometimes been contradictory. See *The Witnesses*; Harold Weisberg, *Selections From Whitewash.* New York: Carroll and Graf, 1994, pp. 284, 518-519; Robert Groden and Harrison Livingstone, *High Treason.* New York: Berkley, 1990, pp. 50-51; *JFK: The Case For Conspiracy*. Boothwyn, PA: New Frontier Video, 1993.

[75] Charles Carrico is part of the Denton Establishment, his father James Carrico having been the longtime Chair of the Chemistry Department at NTSU. Even today, outstanding undergraduates in Chemistry receive the J.L. Carrico Award for their scholastic efforts. See *North Texas Daily*, Special Awards edition, April 1996, p. 6.

[76] William Manchester, *Death of a President*. New York: Harper and Row, 1967, p. 317.

[77] *Ibid*, p. 318.

[78] *North Texan*, October 1963, p. 3.

[79] *Current Biography*, January 1966, pp. 285-288.

[80] *Campus Chat*, December 13, 1963, p. 6.

[81] Manchester, <u>ibid</u>, pp. 341-348, 402-414, 473-481.

[82] DeLloyd Guth and David Wrone, *The Assassination of John F. Kennedy: A Comprehensive Historical and Legal Bibliography*. Westport: Greenwood Press, 1980, p. xiii; Peter Dale Scott, *Deep Politics and the Assassination of JFK*. Berkeley: University of California Press, 1993, p. 46.

[83] Edward J. Epstein, *Inquest*. New York: Viking, 1966.

[84] "Memories of North Texas," Spring Commencement Address, University of North Texas, May 14, 1988.

[85] *Student and Faculty Directory of North Texas State College*, Fall, 1956, p. 55; *The Yucca*, 1958, p. 48.

[86] *North Texan*, May 1967, p. 14. Howard is listed as a graduating senior in the 1958 *Yucca*, but the alumni newsletter has also listed him as a 1960 graduate and on another occasion as a 1961 graduate.

[87] *Ibid.*

[88] Oswald, 1967, pp. 139-140, 147-150, 152-158, 166-167.

[89] Russell, p. 615; Peter Dale Scott, pp. 287-289.

[90] The unbridled civic hucksterism of the city fathers peaked with the effort to entice Dave Letterman to establish a "home office" for his late night TV show in Denton, as a way to

unashamedly brag about the musical roots of Letterman's former Dentonite sidekick, Paul Shaffer. The city also cashed in as much as it could on the wave of national press coverage of the band Deep Blue Something, which launched its career at a local collegiate watering hole called Rick's Place.

[91] The *Record-Chronicle* has rarely done more than to simply acknowledge the anniversary of the assassination with a picture on the front page and an obligatory brief *AP* wire story or two. Speakers who lecture on the assassination have rarely been invited to Denton and those that accept invitations play to small audiences. When researcher Bob Harris appeared at the University of North Texas in November 1994, his visit went unacknowledged by the local press, and despite efforts of the University's Union Program Council to incite interest among students and staff, the lecture was attended by only about 100 people.

The city may not be interested, but surprising and interesting leads continue to surface here. Harry B. Slack and family of

Denton signed in at the Atomic Energy Commission Museum in Oak Ridge, Tennessee on July 26, 1963. They appear to have been part of a Texas group traveling by bus that visited the museum. Readers of Jerry Rose's "Oak Ridge Boy" (*Fourth Decade*, Volume 1, Number 6, September 1994, pp. 15-17) can see that five spaces below the Slacks' inscription on the visitor's log is the infamous "Lee H. Oswald, USSR, Dallas Rd., Dalls, TX." I contacted the Slacks – who still live in Denton – in March 1995 for comment, sending them a copy of the log. They have not yet replied to my inquiry.

[92] *University of North Texas Alumni Directory*, 1994, p. vii.

[93] *North Texas State University Student Directory*, Fall, 1963, pp. 16 and 51. The two men lived at 1423 Panhandle Street.

[94] *Who's Who In America*, 1996, p. 447.

[95] *University of North Texas Alumni Directory*, 1994, pp. v. – vii.

[96] *North Texan*, Spring, 1996, p. 18.

[97] Peter Dale Scott, p. 7.

[98] *University of North Texas Alumni Directory*, 1994, p. v.

www.ingramcontent.com/pod-product-compliance
Lightning Source LLC
Chambersburg PA
CBHW060227290526
45789CB00003B/1442